CELEB ★ ★
POP STAR

CLARE HIBBERT

SEA-TO-SEA
Mankato Collingwood London

This edition first published in 2012 by

Sea-to-Sea Publications
Distributed by Black Rabbit Books
P.O. Box 3263, Mankato, Minnesota 56002

Printed in China

9 8 7 6 5 4 3 2

Published by arrangement with the
Watts Publishing Group Ltd, London.

A CIP catalog record for this book
is available from the Library of Congress.

ISBN: 978-1-59771-333-7

Planning and production by Discovery Books Limited
Managing editor: Laura Durman
Editor: Clare Hibbert
Designer: D.R. ink
Picture research: Colleen Ruck
Thanks to Lauren Ferguson and Danielle Huson

Photo acknowledgements: Getty Images: cover (M. Caulfield/WireImage), pp 4–5 (Chris Gordon), 6 (Dave M. Benett), 8–9 (Brian Ach/WireImage), 10 and 31 (Frank Micelotta/AMA), 11 (Andy Sheppard/Redferns), 12 (Jay West/WireImage), 14–15 (Bill Pugliano), 16 (Frank Micelotta/Universal Music), 16–17 (Frank Micelotta), 18–19 (Theo Wargo/WireImage), 20–21 (Jo Hale), 22 (Richard E. Aaron/Redferns), 26 (Jeff Kravitz/FilmMagic), 29 (Larry Busacca/WireImage); Rex Features: pp 8 (ITV), 24 (Brian Rasic), 28 (Sipa Press); Shutterstock Images: pp 1 and 23 (digitalsport-photoagency), 3 (Kuzma), 13 (beaucroft), 25 (Steven Cashmore).

To the best of its knowledge, the Publisher believes the facts in this book to be true at the time of going to press. However, due to the nature of celebrity, it is impossible to guarantee that all the facts will still be current at the time of reading.

February 2011
RD/6000006415/001

CONTENTS

"It wasn't about how good you could play your instrument, it was about how much you enjoyed playing your instrument." NATHAN

KINGS OF LEON

Many people dream of finding fame as a pop star, either as a solo artist or in a band. It can be a glamorous life, and there's the satisfaction of performing songs that please huge audiences—but it's hard work, too!

Fact

Leon is the name of Nathan, Caleb, and Jared's father.

Dates of birth Nathan Followill June 26, 1979, Caleb Followill January 14, 1982, Matthew Followill September 10, 1984, Jared Followill November 20, 1986

Origins Nashville, Tennessee

Musical style Alternative rock

Influences Led Zeppelin, Rolling Stones, Neil Young, Johnny Cash

Albums *Youth and Young Manhood* (2003), *Aha Shake Heartbreak* (2005), *Because of the Times* (2007), *Only by the Night* (2008)

Achievements Two BRIT Awards and one Grammy Award

Making Pop Music

Pop bands appeared in the 1950s. As well as a singer, there would be a guitarist, bass player, drummer, and, sometimes, a piano player. Today, synthesizers, drum machines, sequencers, and samplers allow new ways of making music.

Grunge and Guitars

Real instruments are still essential for an authentic rock sound. Kings of Leon use not one but three guitars for their energetic brand of grungy rock. Lead guitar is played by Matthew, rhythm guitar by Caleb, and bass by Jared. Nathan accompanies on the drums.

A Musical Childhood

Nathan, Caleb, and Jared are brothers, raised on the road because their father was a traveling preacher. The boys learned to sing and play along to gospel songs. Music has always been part of their lives.

Steps to Fame

Nathan and Caleb started the band, and soon Jared and cousin Matthew joined them. The band signed to record label RCA in 2002. Kings of Leon found instant success in the UK, but fame was slower to come in their native United States. Performing as a support to such big names as U2 and Bob Dylan helped bring them to a wider audience.

www.kingsofleon.com *And, if you like this... check out*
The Strokes www.thestrokes.com *and the Arctic Monkeys* www.arcticmonkeys.com

LILY ALLEN

Undiscovered bands and musicians focus enormous amounts of energy on the quest for a record deal. Without one, they may never make it as a pop star. Some artists, like Lily Allen, are also using the Internet to promote their music.

What Labels Do

Record labels, such as Lily's label Regal Recordings, are companies that market music. They pay to produce CDs and distribute them to stores and other retailers. They also help sell them. Publicists set up interviews with the media and make sure that new tracks are played on the radio and TV.

Finding Talent

Record labels employ talent scouts (or A&R executives) to seek out tomorrow's big names. They go to gigs on the lookout for talent and listen to sample tracks (demos) sent in by wannabe stars like Allen.

Lily Online

Lily Allen signed up with Regal Recordings in 2005, but before long she lost patience with the slow progress of her first album. Lily posted demos and mixtapes on her MySpace page to whip up interest. It worked, and her album release gained momentum. Lily still uses the Internet to promote herself and to give details of "secret" gigs.

Into the Future

Other artists are using the web to bypass record labels altogether. Now that music can be put online, available for anyone to download, will labels be able to survive?

Fact

Lily Allen sang in her school's chamber choir and achieved grade 8 in singing. She can play the piano, violin, guitar, and trumpet!

Celeb bio

Date of birth May 2, 1984

Place of birth London, UK

Musical style Pop and pop rock

Influences Blondie, T-Rex, Squeeze, The Clash

Albums *Alright, Still* (2006), *It's Not Me, It's You* (2009)

TV show *Lily Allen and Friends*

Achievements Three BRIT Award nominations and one Grammy nomination

Famous relative The actor, Keith Allen, is Lily's father

"I had been doing demos and I probably had, like, seven or eight that I was confident enough to put on [MySpace] for people to hear."

Lily's MySpace page.

www.lilyallenmusic.com *And, if you like this… check out* *Pixie Lott* www.pixielott.com *or Little Boots* www.littlebootsmusic.co.uk

7

LEONA LEWIS

Televised talent contests are popular all over the world. Shows like *The X Factor*, *Fame Academy*, and *American Idol* search to find the next new pop sensation, offering the prize of a record contract. Superstar Leona Lewis was discovered this way.

Would-be Stars

Thousands of people audition for TV talent shows. More than 180,000 wannabes came forward for the latest series of *The X Factor*—with only a dozen contestants making it through to the live shows.

Celebrity Judges

Various celebrities and music moguls have acted as judges on reality TV contests. Simon Cowell is the best known, with a reputation for harsh criticism. Cheryl Cole, who made her name fronting Girls Aloud, is another. Sharon Osbourne of *The Osbournes*, record producer Pete Waterman, and Spice Girl Geri Halliwell have also all been judges at one time or another.

X Factor Winner

Leona Lewis is one of the most successful stars to have been discovered on reality TV. Her good looks, charm, and amazing vocals won the hearts of the viewers, who voted for her in their thousands. Even Simon Cowell said, "I think she's one of the best singers we've seen in this country for a long, long time!"

Recording Success

Cowell signed Leona to his label, SyCo, and lined up some of the top people in the business to work with her on her album, *Spirit*. "Bleeding Love," taken from that album, was the best-selling single of 2007 in the UK and of 2008 in the United States.

"I feel really lucky that I have got Simon who believes in me. The show gave me a lot of experience and made me more self-confident."

Leona with Simon Cowell and Shayne Ward. Shayne won *The X Factor* in 2005.

Celeb bio

Date of birth **April 3, 1985**

Place of birth **London, UK**

Claim to fame **Winning series 3 of** *The X Factor*

Musical style **Pop and R & B**

Influences **Whitney Houston, Mariah Carey, Eva Cassidy**

Albums *Spirit* **(2007),** *Echo* **(2009)**

Achievements **Six BRIT Award nominations and three Grammy Award nominations**

www.leonalewismusic.co.uk *And, if you like this… check out*
Mariah Carey www.mariahcarey.com *and Alesha Dixon* www.aleshadixon.co.uk

9

SONGWRITING
NE-YO

Writing the perfect pop song is truly an art. Some are a joint effort by a composer, responsible for the music, and a lyricist, who comes up with the words. Talented songwriters like Ne-Yo write both the music and the lyrics.

Writing Work

When performing artists write their own songs, they are known as singer-songwriters. However, in the world of pop, a great many bands and singers perform songs that are the work of professional songwriters, employed by the record label.

A Career Writing Songs

Ne-Yo started writing songs in his late teens, coming up with songs for the short-lived boy band, Youngstown. He went on to pen hits for such big stars as Mary J. Blige and Faith Evans. He also cowrote one of the biggest hits of 2004, Mario's "Let Me Love You." Shortly after, Ne-Yo was signed to the record label Def Jam as an artist in his own right.

Solo Albums

Ne-Yo wrote the lyrics for every song on his debut album, *In My Own Words*. It sold more than two million copies worldwide. The hit "So Sick" reached Number One in both the United States and the UK. Ne-Yo's second and third albums also both went platinum (they sold more than a million copies each).

Other Hits

Ne-Yo hasn't given up writing for other stars, often collaborating with Stargate, a Norwegian songwriting team. He has penned tracks for Leona Lewis, Corbin Bleu, and Enrique Iglesias, and was responsible for Rihanna's hits "Unfaithful" and "Take a Bow" and Beyoncé's "Irreplaceable."

Celeb bio

Real name **Shaffer Chimere Smith**

Date of birth **October 18, 1982**

Place of birth **Camden, Arkansas**

Musical style **Pop and R & B**

Influences **Sammy Davis, Jr., Babyface, Michael Jackson**

Albums ***In My Own Words*** (2006), ***Because of You*** (2007), ***Year of the Gentleman*** (2008)

Achievements **Three Grammy Awards and two MOBO Awards**

Ne-Yo duets with Rihanna at the American Music Awards.

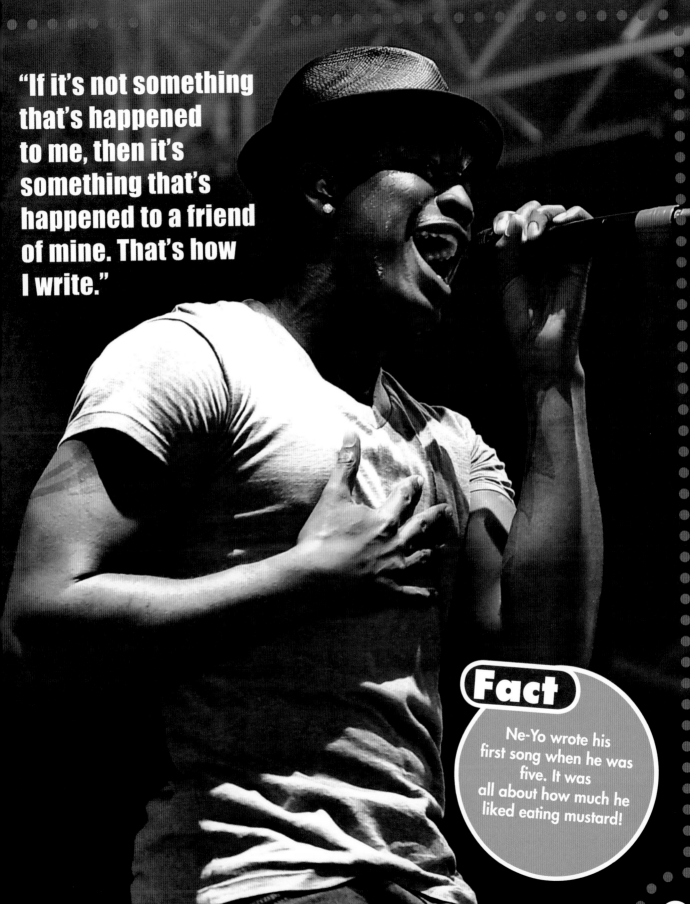

"If it's not something that's happened to me, then it's something that's happened to a friend of mine. That's how I write."

Fact

Ne-Yo wrote his first song when he was five. It was all about how much he liked eating mustard!

Celeb bio

Date of birth June 8, 1977

Place of birth Atlanta, Georgia

Musical style Hip-hop, pop, and R & B

Influences Wu-Tang Clan, Pete Rock, Michael Jackson

Albums *The College Dropout* (2004), *Late Registration* (2005), *Graduation* (2007), *808s & Heartbreak* (2008)

Achievements Three BRIT Awards from six nominations and 12 Grammy Awards from 30 nominations

> "The beats are what catches someone's ear and makes a record a hit."

KANYE WEST

When artists record a new track, they rely heavily on the studio's record producer to make it sound good. Some artists, such as Kanye West, are talented producers as well as performers.

Studio Time

Recording studios are specially designed for recording music. There's a soundproofed live room, where the artist or band performs. The control room is where the record producer records and mixes the sound.

Producing a Record

Producers, such as Kanye, record songs on a multitrack recorder, and then use a mixing console to adjust different aspects of the sound. West often uses samplers (machines that "steal" musical sounds from existing recordings) and sequencers (machines that help to order digital music) to produce a rich and interesting sound.

Production Breakthrough

Although Kanye West is known as an artist in his own right, he started out as a producer. In 2001 he worked on Jay-Z's classic hip hop album, *The Blueprint*, which made sampling popular again. Kanye produced four of the 13 tracks, and put in samples from The Doors, David Bowie, and The Jackson 5, among others.

Studio Albums

Following the success of *The Blueprint*, Roc-A-Fella Records gave Kanye a record deal. His first three albums each won a Grammy for Best Rap Album. In his experimental fourth album, Kanye moved away from rap and made heavy use of his Roland TR-808 drum machine, giving his music a much slicker, more synthetic sound.

Fact

Kenny West, a cartoon character based on Kanye, made his debut in *The Cleveland Show* in the fall of 2009. Kanye did the voiceover.

The mixing console has controls that are used to blend the levels of instruments and vocals on the tracks.

DANCE ROUTINES

Some bands are as famous for their dance routines as for their music. Stars even invent their own moves – Madonna came up with the vogue, for instance. An exciting dance routine helps hold the audience's interest.

Sassy Sequences

Some performers improvise as they go along, but most stars use moves that have been planned out beforehand. Often these are the work of a professional choreographer. Choreographers come up with a sequence of moves that flow into each other and really complement the music.

Girl Bands

Many all-girl bands are famous for their choreography. Everyone in the group practices so they can all perform identical moves in perfect time. American girl band Pussycat Dolls actually started out as a dance troupe, rather than a pop group!

> "I've trained for this all my life. I did tap dancing, jazz, and ballet." KIMBERLY WYATT

PUSSYCAT DOLLS

The Dolls

Choreographer Robin Antin formed Pussycat Dolls in 1995. It was a burlesque dance act—the girls dressed up in old-fashioned corsets and danced along to guest singers. Guest Dolls have included Christina Aguilera, Gwen Stefani, Pink and Scarlett Johansson. Their performances in Hollywood were extremely popular.

The Move to Pop

In 2003, Robin launched the Dolls as a pop group. Nicole Scherzinger joined as lead singer along with another vocalist, Melody Thornton. The other members were all talented dancers. Pussycat Dolls released their first album in 2005 and a second successful album, *Doll Domination,* followed in 2008. However, the Dolls were dogged by rumors of tension over Scherzinger's role in the band. In 2009, the Dolls opted to take a break from recording, and in 2010, it was confirmed that all of the Pussycat Dolls apart from Scherzinger were leaving the band.

Celeb bio

Dates of birth Nicole Scherzinger June 29, 1978, Melody Thornton September 28, 1984, Ashley Roberts September 14, 1981, Jessica Sutta May 15, 1982, Kimberly Wyatt February 4, 1982

Origins Los Angeles, California

Musical style Dance pop

Influences En Vogue, Spice Girls, Christina Aguilera

Albums *PCD* (2005), *Doll Domination* (2008)

Achievements One Grammy Award nomination

Fact

The routine for "Thriller" by Michael Jackson remains one of the most popular of all time. In May 2009, a world record was broken when 242 people performed the routine together.

www.pcdmusic.com *And, if you like this... check out Girlicious* www.girliciousmusic.com *and The Saturdays* www.thesaturdays.co.uk

15

VIDEOS
RIHANNA

ABOVE: Rihanna being filmed for the "Hate That I Love You" video. MAIN PICTURE: Rihanna in the video for "We Ride."

Fact

The most expensive video ever made was for 30 Seconds to Mars' song "From Yesterday." It cost nearly $13 million to produce and was shot in China.

Videos are a fantastic way to promote music. They give fans a chance to see their idol perform without the need to go to a live gig. Twenty-four-hour music TV has been around for years, but now YouTube and similar web sites have made videos more accessible than ever. Videos by stars such as Rihanna get thousands of YouTube hits every day.

Celeb bio

Full name **Robyn Rihanna Fenty**
Date of birth **February 20, 1988**
Place of birth **Saint Michael, Barbados**
Musical style **R & B, soul, and pop**
Influences **Destiny's Child, Brandy, Lady Saw**
Albums ***Music of the Sun*** (2005), ***A Girl Like Me*** (2006), ***Good Girl Gone Bad*** (2007)
Achievements **One BRIT Award nomination and one Grammy Award from nine nominations**

Video Styles

The simplest videos just show the artist playing or singing the song. Others showcase slick dance routines. Rihanna's early music videos were quite simple. For "Pon de Replay", she sings and dances in the studio and in a club.

Directors

Videos can be works of art in themselves, making use of special effects, atmospheric locations, and even animation. Several feature movie directors, such as Michel Gondry, who started out working on music videos. Rihanna's favorite director is Anthony Mandler, who has made more than half of her music videos. Mandler strives to tell a story through each video he directs.

Winning Awards

Rihanna's videos are incredibly popular on YouTube, probably because they are like mini movies. They have been nominated for, and won, several awards. The "Umbrella" video, in which Chris Applebaum came up with the idea of covering Rihanna in silver paint, was nominated for four awards and won an MTV Video Music Award and a MuchMusic Video Award. Applebaum also received a nomination for Best Video Director.

"It was a pretty cool thing to do. I never thought that in a million years I would paint myself up to my nostrils in silver and do a video."

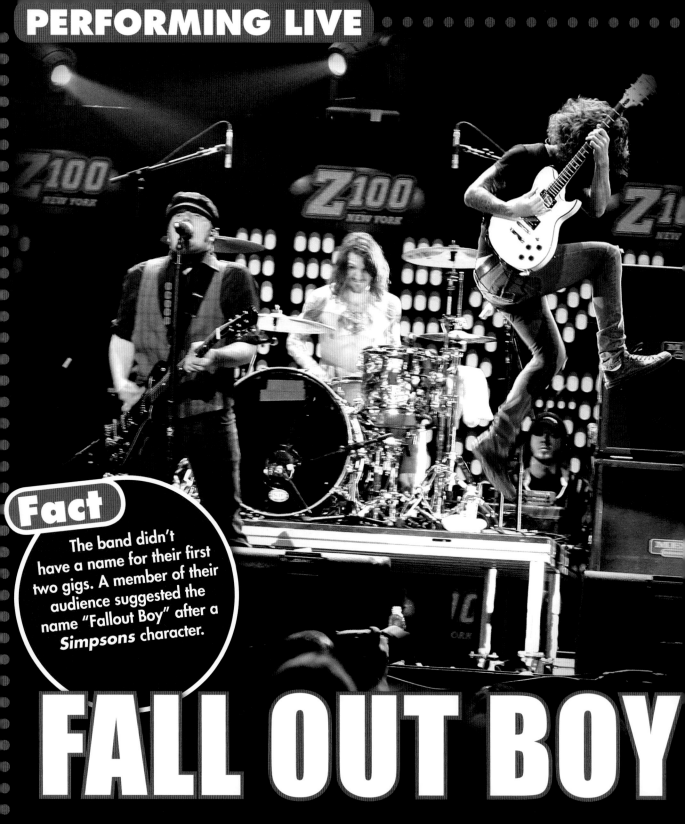

FALL OUT BOY

Whoever heard of a shy performing artist? Most stars really enjoy getting in touch with their fans. Whether the venue's a bar, a sports stadium, or a festival stage, live performance gives the chance to get feedback from the listeners who really matter.

"Connecting with the crowd is the best part."
PATRICK

"I just like performing—it just feels good." PETE

Celeb bio

Dates of birth Patrick Stump April 27, 1984, Joe Trohman September 1, 1984, Pete Wentz June 5, 1979, Andy Hurley May 31, 1980

Origins Wilmette, Illinois

Musical style Pop punk

Influences The Smiths, Bad Religion, New Found Glory, Elvis Costello

Albums *From Under the Cork Tree* (2005), *Infinity on High* (2007), *Folie à Deux* (2008)

Achievements One Grammy Award nomination, two MTV Video Music Awards, and two *Kerrang!* awards

Small Shows

Many bands start out by playing small gigs at local venues. It's a way to test new material and, perhaps, catch the eye—or ear!—of an A&R executive. Once a band is signed to a label, live shows are a much more organized affair.

Starting Out

Fall Out Boy started out in the suburbs of Chicago in the early 2000s. They released demos to fans and played gigs throughout the city, until they attracted the interest of a major label—Island Records.

On Tour

Once established, bands like Fall Out Boy go on tour as a way to promote their latest album. Sometimes bands are on the road for months. Often they play the same set each night, just in a different city. It can be exhausting!

Folie Tour

In 2008 and 2009, Fall Out Boy played dates in the Americas, Europe, South Africa, East Asia, Australia, and New Zealand to promote their *Folie à Deux* album. In October 2008, they headlined the first BBC Switch Live concert ever in London—a gig specially targeted at teenage pop fans. They also played a secret gig inside the London Dungeon for 80 members of their fan club.

www.falloutboyrock.com *And, if you like this... check out*
Boys Like Girls *www.boyslikegirls.com and My Chemical Romance www.mychemicalromance.com*

19

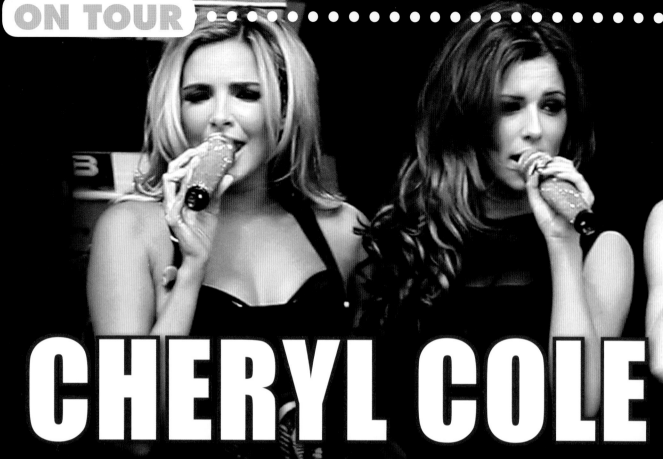

CHERYL COLE

The biggest pop successes tour the world playing to their fans. First-class travel on planes, trains, and tour buses becomes a way of life. Home comforts are replaced by restaurant meals, takeouts, and hotel beds.

Location, Location

In most countries top venues for tour dates include arenas, stadiums, city halls, and theaters. There are also pop and rock festivals globally. There's the UK's Glastonbury Festival, and in the U.S,. the Siren Music Festival on Coney Island in Brooklyn, NY.

Touring Queens

Cheryl Cole has had plenty of experience of life on the road as part of the record-breaking girl band, Girls Aloud. Over the years, Girls Aloud have clocked up five long tours, performing to hundreds of thousands of excited fans. In 2006, the girls documented the runup to their Chemistry tour in a six-part series for TV channel E4. The program revealed that life on the road is not always that glamorous!

Solo Star

Cheryl is now experiencing performing and touring as a singer in her own right. In 2009, Girls Aloud took a break to focus on solo projects. Cheryl released her own album, *3 Words*, in October 2009, and performed the first single "Fight for This Love" live on the *X Factor*, where she was also a judge. In 2010, Cheryl was the opening act on the Black Eyed Peas' European tour, bringing her music to fans across Europe and the UK.

Popular Girl

Although life on the road can be grueling, touring really helps to boost sales and can raise a pop star's profile. Despite Cheryl's personal setbacks, including a difficult and very public breakup with her husband Ashley Cole, *3 Words* stormed straight to Number One in the UK charts.

Girls Aloud play at the V Festival in 2008.

Celeb bio

Date of birth **June 30, 1983**

Place of birth **Newcastle-upon-Tyne, UK**

Claim to fame **Having more than 20 Top Ten singles in a row with Girls Aloud**

Musical style **Dance pop**

Influences **Kylie Minogue, Spice Girls**

Albums ***Sound of the Underground*** **(2003),** ***What Will the Neighbors Say?*** **(2004),** ***Chemistry*** **(2005),** ***Tangled Up*** **(2007),** ***Out of Control*** **(2008),** ***3 Words*** **(2009)**

Achievements **One BRIT Award out of four nominations**

"I saw will.i.am the other day and he got me really excited about the tour… It's just incredible, it still doesn't feel quite real yet."

Fact

Girls Aloud's Tangled Up tour in 2008 cost more than $5 million to stage. The girls had four costume changes during the set!

www.cherylcole.com *And, if you like this… check out* Sugababes *www.sugababes.com and Katy Perry* www.katyperry.com

Celeb bio

Date of birth **August 16, 1958**

Place of birth **Bay City, Michigan**

Claim to fame **Three decades of superstardom**

Musical style **Pop and rock**

Influences **Nancy Sinatra, The Supremes, William Orbit**

Key albums ***Like a Virgin*** **(1984),** ***True Blue*** **(1986),** ***The Immaculate Collection*** **(1990),** ***Erotica*** **(1992),** ***Confessions on a Dance Floor*** **(2005),** ***Hard Candy*** **(2008)**

Achievements **Two BRIT Awards and seven Grammy Awards from 29 nominations**

1983

MADONNA

"I am a survivor. I am like a cockroach —you just can't get rid of me."

To have real staying power, stars need to be able to reinvent themselves. Their sound usually changes direction over time. Their image can evolve too—it can be as simple as getting a haircut or wearing new outfits.

"Queen of Pop"

Madonna is the most successful female pop star of all time. During a career spanning more than 30 years, she has sold around 200 million albums—and updated her image many times. Her early look was big blonde hair, vintage dresses, and men's dinner jackets, worn with lots of bracelets and necklaces. By the time of her third album, *True Blue*, she was styled like a 1940's Hollywood diva.

Shifting Styles

Since those early years, Madonna has regularly changed her look. She has appeared clad in black leather or dressed as a rhinestone-loving cowgirl. And at one point she styled herself as one of her heroines, Marilyn Monroe.

Musical Successes

Madonna's singing and music have also evolved over the years. She has released more than 20 albums, including studio albums, live albums, compilations, and movie soundtracks. *Like a Virgin* and *The Immaculate Collection* each sold more than 10 million copies in the United States alone.

2008

Madonna on her "Sticky and Sweet" tour.

Staying in Shape

People either love or hate Madonna's trim, athletic figure. To maintain her image, she follows a strict diet and works out in the gym for more than two hours each day. Whatever people think, Madonna is in great shape. Performers half her age would have trouble keeping up with her energetic stage performances!

THE FANS

Where would celebrities be without their fans? Diehard fans buy every musical release and attend every live performance. They spend their hard-earned cash on all sorts of merchandise, including T-shirts, bags, buttons, and books.

Celeb bio

Dates of birth will.i.am March 15, 1975, apl.de.ap November 28, 1974, Taboo July 14, 1975, Fergie March 27, 1975

Origins **Los Angeles, California**

Musical style **Hip-hop**

Influences **Stevie Wonder, James Brown, A Tribe Called Quest, De La Soul**

Albums ***Behind the Front*** (1998), ***Elephunk*** (2003), ***Monkey Business*** (2005), ***The E.N.D.*** (2009)

Achievements **Three Grammy Awards from 10 nominations**

Official Web Sites

Most pop stars have an official web site. This is the place for fans to check out tour dates, listen to a preview of the latest single, or download photos. Band members may also write a blog to keep fans in touch with what they are doing.

Fan Sites

Sometimes fans run their own sites. Like official sites, these may have biographies of the band members and pictures or videos. There might be an online chat area where likeminded fans can discuss the latest band-related news. Social networking sites also have pages dedicated to fans of particular artists.

New Departure

In 2008, American hip-hop band Black Eyed Peas helped launch Dipdive, a different kind of web site, which they called a lifestyle engine. Among other things, they used it to upload a video supporting Barack Obama's presidential campaign. Sites such as Dipdive allow fans much more interactivity.

About Black Eyed Peas

Black Eyed Peas already had a couple of rap albums to their name when female singer Fergie joined them for their breakthrough album, *Elephunk*, which included the hit "Where Is the Love?" Her soulful vocals were a perfect match for the group's slick, hip-hop sound. In 2009, the band achieved their first American Number One single with "Boom Boom Pow."

"We planned on being global from the very beginning."
WILL.I.AM

Black Eyed Peas performing for fans at the UK's Glastonbury Festival in 2009.

BLACK EYED PEAS

Black Eyed Peas perform at the Live 8 Philadelphia Concert with Rita Marley and Stephen Marley.

http://blackeyedpeas.dipdive.com *And, if you like this… check out Flo Rida* www.officialflo.com *and Timbaland* www.timbalandmusic.com

"I'm so honored and I'm so humbled by this award."
AT THE 2007 AMERICAN MUSIC AWARDS

Fact

Beyoncé is an acclaimed actress and received a Golden Globe nomination for her role in *Dreamgirls*.

BEYONCÉ

Awards such as the Grammy Awards, the BRITs, and MTV Music Video Awards give recognition to pop stars—and the chance for a glitzy party. There are also categories to reward the people behind the scenes.

Star Performer

Beyoncé has won seven Grammy Awards as a solo artist and three more as part of the band Destiny's Child. Grammy Awards are the American music industry's top awards.

UK Talent

The BRITs are presented in February each year by the British record industry. They include awards for the best British male artist, female artist, group, single, album, live act, new act, and producer. There are also awards for the best international acts. Beyoncé won a BRIT for best international female solo artist in 2004.

About Beyoncé

Beyoncé is one of the world's most successful female artists. She's been a solo artist since 2003, but she began her career in 1990 with Destiny's Child, the world's best-selling female group. One of her proudest moments was performing at the Lincoln Memorial in January 2009 to mark Barack Obama becoming the first black president of the United States.

Superstar Skills

Beyoncé's success is based on her powerful, mezzo-soprano voice. She has cowritten almost all of the songs she has sung and also helped out with the studio production. Add to that her great beauty and her talent as an actress, and it's no wonder Beyoncé has won more than 100 awards!

Celeb bio

Date of birth **September 4, 1981**
Place of birth **Houston, Texas**
Claim to fame **Previously the lead singer of Destiny's Child**
Musical style **R & B and pop**
Influences **Aretha Franklin, Whitney Houston, Mary J. Blige, Donna Summer, Mariah Carey**
Albums ***Dangerously in Love*** **(2003),** ***B'Day*** **(2006),** ***I Am... Sasha Fierce*** **(2008)**
Achievements **First female artist to have a Number One single ("Crazy in Love") and album (*Dangerously in Love*) in both the U.S. and UK charts**

music awards

Beyoncé has won all the most prestigious awards in the music business. They include:

American Music Awards Decided by viewers of the ABC network, presented each November

Billboard Music Awards Presented by the American music magazine *Billboard* each December

BRIT Awards Presented each February by the British record business; categories include Best British Album

Grammy Awards Presented each January by the U.S. record business; categories include Record of the Year and Album of the Year

MTV Video Music Awards Presented each September by music channel MTV for the best music videos

www.beyonceonline.com *And, if you like this... check out*
Mary J. Blige www.mjblige.com *and Jennifer Hudson* www.jenniferhudsononline.com

Celeb bio

Date of birth January 31, 1981

Place of birth Memphis, Tennessee,

Claim to fame Previously the lead singer of 'N Sync

Musical style R & B, soul, and pop

Influences Elton John, Michael Jackson, Stevie Wonder

Albums *Justified* (2002), *FutureSex/LoveSounds* (2006)

Achievements Three BRIT Awards from five nominations and six Grammy Awards from 26 nominations

Justin on the catwalk at a show for his range of denimwear.

JUSTIN TIMBERLAKE

Celebrities who've made their name in the world of pop often branch out into other fields. Sometimes the results are downright embarrassing! Other times, that star quality shines through whether the platform is acting, modeling, or doing something completely different.

Justin's Music

Justin Timberlake is one pop star who has moved effortlessly through a range of careers. After starting out on the small screen, he found fame as part of the boy band 'N Sync. 'N Sync's last album, *Celebrity*, sold more than 10 million copies worldwide.

Solo Career

Since the band split, Justin has had the most successful career of the five 'N Syncers. His first solo album was released in 2002, followed by *FutureSex/LoveSounds* in 2006. Justin has also collaborated with various big-name stars, including Madonna, Ciara, and Timbaland.

Product Promotion

Alongside his music, Justin has earned money from sponsorship deals, appearing in ads for McDonald's and Budweiser, among others. He owns his own brand of tequila, 901, and in the past has co-owned restaurants in Hollywood and New York.

Films and Fashion

Justin's many movie roles have included being the voice of Artie in *Shrek the Third* and *Shrek Goes Fourth*. Justin is no stranger to the world of fashion, either. In 2005, he co-launched his designer denimwear range, William Rast. A popular special guest at fashion shows, he has famously shared the catwalk with supermodel Gisele Bündchen.

"If you're going to do something, go ahead and throw 115 percent at it."

www.justintimberlake.com *And, if you like this... check out Robbie Williams* www.robbiewilliams.com *and Jesse McCartney* www.jessemac.com

29

GLOSSARY

A&R Short for "Artists and Repertoire." An A&R executive's job is to find new talent and then to support artists, helping them to record their music and keep a good relationship with the record label.

animation A motion picture, sometimes called a cartoon, that shows successive still images (or computer-generated images) very quickly, so that characters appear to be moving.

bassist Someone who plays bass guitar.

burlesque A provocative dance act, sometimes involving striptease. The female performers are scantily clad, often in old-fashioned underwear, such as corsets and stockings.

chamber choir A group of five to 15 singers of classical music.

choreographer Someone whose job is to plan out dance routines.

collaborate Work together with.

demo Short for "demonstration." A recording that gives a taste of the sort of music an artist can make.

distribute Supply goods to retailers.

drum machine An electronic instrument that mimics the sound of a drum kit and produces percussive sounds in programmable beats.

gig Another word for concert.

gospel A kind of Christian music based on African-American folk, with strong rhythms and powerful choruses, combining elements from other forms of music, including spirituals, blues, and jazz.

grungy Describes a style of rock music with noisy guitars and quiet, mumbled vocals.

lifestyle engine A web site that provides a platform for artists to connect directly with their fans. Instead of just posting content, such as gig dates or other news, a lifestyle engine claims to allow fans and bands to truly interact.

lyricist Someone who writes lyrics (words).

mixing console Also called a mixing desk. A piece of electronic equipment that allows sound signals to be combined to make music.

mogul An important or powerful person.

multitrack recorder A machine for recording different parts of a piece of music as several "tracks" of sound, for example, a vocal track, a lead guitar track, and so on. Using this method, each track can be changed independently later on, for example, replacing the vocals or making them louder.

platinum Describes a recording that has sold more than a million copies.

promote Help to create publicity for.

publicist Someone responsible for promoting something.

pyrotechnics Special effects that involve fireworks.

R & B Short for "Rhythm and Blues." A form of popular music with its origins in African-American music—blues with jazz rhythms.

reality TV An unscripted TV show starring people (being themselves, not acting) facing challenges, such as living together in a house, taking part in a talent contest, or trying out a new job.

record label A company that produces recorded music.

record producer Someone who supervises the making of a musical recording, responsible for turning the recorded sounds into a finished work.

retailer A seller of products, for example, a store.

sampler A machine that takes sounds from existing recordings so they can be used in new music.

sequencer A machine that is used to help order or compose electronic music.

solo artist Someone who performs alone, rather than as part of a band.

synthesizer An electronic instrument used to make different sounds. Most synthesizers have a keyboard. They can imitate other instruments or produce unique, new sounds.

talent contest A competition that rewards the most gifted contestant.

venue The place where something, for example, a concert, happens.

FURTHER INFORMATION

BOOKS

Livewire Real Lives: Madonna by Julia Holt (Hodder Murray, 2004)

Pop Culture, A View from the Paparazzi: Justin Timberlake by Jim Whiting (Mason Crest, 2007)

Raintree Freestyle Star Files: Beyoncé Knowles by Nicola Hodgson (Raintree, 2005)

super-activ: Pop Music by Nicole Carmichael (Hodder Children's Books, 2000)

Trailblazers: How to be a Pop Star by David Orme (Ransom Publishing, 2006)

WEB SITES

http://www.grammy.com
The official website of the Grammy Awards, the annual awards from the U.S. record industry.

http://www.brits.co.uk
The official website of the BRIT Awards, the annual pop awards from the British record industry.

http://www.mtv.com/music/artist
The official website of the television channel MTV, with music videos for a variety of pop stars.

http://www.rollingstone.com/artists
A directory of pop artists from *Rolling Stone* magazine.

http://www.americanidol.com
The official website of the U.S. reality TV show.